your faith. I found this chapter to be well written, informative and personally relevant and I highly recommend this book.

~ *Mr. Carl Steven, MBA* ~
Business Owner and Entrepreneur

In chapter 5, Walk By Faith, Mrs. Taylor lays out the practical ways in which we can learn to walk by faith. Spending time with God and being strengthened and empowered in His presence allows us to walk by faith. This chapter serves as a guide and gives several scripture references to further prove this point. Lastly, please remember this, ***"You see, we cannot walk by faith without the assistance of the Holy Spirit"***. Lean into Him to receive all that you need in this faith walk.

~ *Mrs. Jennifer Nelson* ~

I0457452

Lord Increase My Faith

Faith to Move Mountains

Frizella Taylor

As someone who used to struggle trying to figure it out the Lord's way, and how to put my faith fully into the Lord I enjoyed reading chapter 1: Increase My Faith. You nailed being able to not only answer the question of what is faith but the triggers that come with fully putting your faith in only the Lord. This chapter will be able to fully equip readers who are faith-based as well as nonbelievers with a general idea of what to expect when they let go and just let God.

~ Ms. Diamond L. Bryant, Granddaughter ~

Praise the Lord! I am so excited about Prophetess Frizella Taylor's new book "LORD Increase My FAITH!"

It is a pleasure and opportunity to know Prophetess Taylor for over 25 years. I can truly say that she is a woman who exemplifies relentless faith! She is a lover of God, in all her ways. She is resilient and unwavering in her faith. She knows no defeat in God, because of her faith and trust in God. He always brings her out of whatever situations she faces. Prophetess Taylor always prevail.

This book will be a tremendous blessing to everyone who reads it. It will help you through your personal struggles in life and how to overcome them through Exercising Your Faith and trust in God! Allow this book to help you to develop your faith in God. Prophetess Taylor knows what it takes to be an overcomer in God through Faith. She has written this book with you in mind concerning your victory! After you read this book, God will help you to gain the knowledge needed for your breakthrough to overcome by Faith!

~ Apostle Dr. Dorothy Nelson ~
New Destiny of Faith Kingdom Ministry

Chapter 3 "Stretch My Faith" explores the profound idea of stretching one's faith beyond the visible and tangible. Prophetess Taylor parallels faith growth with muscle strengthening and emphasizes belief in God's promises. Her testimony demonstrates faith's power to move mountains. This must-read book will empower readers to reflect on faith's limitless potential. This is a must-read for faith-strengthening.

~ Dr. Robert L. Watts, Jr. D.Min., M.Ed. ~
"Dr. Rob" CEO/Owner
RLW Empowerment Services, LLC

I absolutely love chapter 4 "Strengthen My Faith". It provided me with what it means to strengthen my faith and the importance of strengthening my prayer life. It helped me to understand that when challenges arise in life praying can change the outcome of the situation.

It outlines the scriptures to pray when challenged in life. I now have a better understanding of how to strengthen my faith and my prayer life.

~Ms. Donnetta Jones, MS, CADC ~
Director of Residential Substance Use Services
Lutheran Social Services of Illinois

In chapter 5 Frizella very clearly and concisely lays out what it means to "Walk By Faith". The chapter defines "Walking by Faith" and how our spiritual growth is connected with our walk with God. She shows us in God's Word that as we grow spiritually we will abandon ungodly cravings and gain assistance in our growth through the Holy Spirit. Frizella wraps up the chapter with key points in building your relationship with God and growing in

Lord Increase My Faith: Faith to Move Mountains

ISBN: 978-1-953526-58-8

Published by TaylorMade Publishing
Jacksonville, FL
www.TaylorMadePublishingFL.com
(904) 323-1334

TaylorMade Publishing

Faith
as small as a
Mustard Seed
can move
Mountains

Matthew 17:20

DEDICATION

This book is dedicated to my awesome family: my husband, Steve, daughter Deliliah and grandkids Levester, III and Diamond and my sister Corean, who has been by my side with each book that I have written, and you are such a fantastic editor. I am so grateful for each of you who has been a part of my writing career and believing in the words the Lord placed in me to share. Thank you all for the shared love and bountiful blessings and dedicated support. I could not do what I am called to do without each of you. I am overly grateful for each of you and the roles you play in my life.

Acknowledgements

My sincere gratitude to:

- My sister Corean for all her hard work and diligence in editing and proofing my manuscripts. Your professionalism is beyond great, with every "I" dotted and every "T" crossed, you leave no stone unturned.
- My brother Joseph you are an awesome sounding board that keeps me grounded in the truth of the Word. You challenge my insights from every side, line upon line and precept upon precept.
- Tanya Greene, my intercessor and Vice President of Women in Progress Ministries, your prayers always keep me strong and encourages me to push forward. No matter what you are going through, you always stop, drop, and pray!
- Cheryl Wilson one of my best friends and biggest encouragers, she truly can take a lemon and make lemonade.
- Tierra Alexander and daughters, a happenstance friendship that has evolved into relationships of spiritual daughter and granddaughters, Nelani and Nevaeh. You all keep me praying and understanding the true call of God for this season of my life.
- Pastor Jason Masters who I am eternally grateful for the season of leadership you provided. Many days of praying together for the church and families, birthed within me an awareness and need for the ministry to further the gospel of Jesus Christ.

- Apostle Charlene Crossley my mother of Zion, you are the epitome of Faith in Action! Your continual leadership influences my life daily from the many lessons and classes you have taught. You are the true example of a woman in ministry!
- Bishop Ed T. Winford words cannot express the gratefulness and appreciation I have for you! You have been an anchor of stability in my life for years. Your wisdom is profound and unmatched. You are a father figure in the absence of my natural father. I am forever thankful for you and your leadership that keeps giving.

Table of Contents

Forward by Bishop Ed T. Winford

I am so excited to share with you a statement of all the jewels in this book. In a language that anyone can understand, Prophetess Frizella Taylor shares in her book "LORD Increase MY Faith", she givesMs a scriptural step-by-step guide on how to increase our faith in God.

In the book, Frizella shares her own faith challenges and difficult times. This book is a must read for anyone who want to increase their faith and be all that God has ordained them to be. Even the most astute believer in Christ will be blessed from reading this book. I highly recommend that you secure a copy of this book, LORD Increase MY Faith.

Frizella is an amazing anointed multi-talented woman of God. She is an author, prophet, teacher, entrepreneur, wife, mother, grandmother, and a former pastor.

Bishop Ed T. Winford, Presiding Bishop Emeritus,
The Kings Agenda

Introduction

Faith, what does that even mean? The dictionary defines faith as:

1. Confidence or trust in a person or thing;
2. Belief that is not based on proof;
3. Belief in God or in the doctrines or teachings of religion.

Christian theology defines faith this way: then trust in God and in HIS promises as made through Jesus Christ and the scriptures by which humans are justified or saved.

Faith is for believers. If your friends and family struggle with believing with you concerning your healing, your business or your relationship; it is simply because they have not received "the measure of faith" Romans 12:3c says, "...God has dealt to each one a measure of faith." When the Bible talks about "the measure of faith," it's not saying that faith is available to everyone in the world, but rather that it's available to believers. As a believer, you have "The measure of faith" which is the same for each believer. This measure of faith is the degree you as a believer can use with the gifts God has given you.

It is the same faith that Jesus has. Individual believers develop and strengthen their faith over time, at different paces, and by the Word of God. However, their faith is no more or different than yours. You have that same opportunity to extend your faith, stretch your faith or increase your faith. Another way of looking at your measure of faith is determined by how much you trust God. Your trust in the Heavenly Father helps you to increase your faith.

Hebrews chapter eleven is what I liken to the "Faith in Action" chapter of the Bible! Hebrews 11:1 Amplified version reads as follows, "Now faith is the assurance (title deed, confirmation) of things hoped for (divinely guaranteed), and the evidence of things not seen [the conviction of their reality—faith comprehends as fact what cannot be experienced by the physical senses]."

What we see here is the action of faith or what faith actually did for many individuals. These individuals had the confidence and trust in God of the Old Testament and Jesus of the New Testament. Faith provides substance to our foundation which in turn is the ultimate foundation of our hope. Faith provides evidence that things that are unseen can for will becomes reality. Such things as forgiveness of sin through the sacrifice of Jesus; evidence that Christ intercession in heaven is on our behalf. Hope speaks to our future while faith speaks to our present, NOW Faith.

For the next few chapters, we will discover how the Lord will help us to increase our faith; how to exercise our faith;

how to stretch our faith; how to strengthen our faith and lastly how to walk by faith.

After each chapter, you will have an opportunity to write out your personal Faith In Action steps to further activate your faith and believe God for the supernatural manifestation of His promises in your life. Simply write out some bullet points or goals to achieve the objective of the completed chapter that will aid you in accomplishing a pattern of growth in your faith.

Example:

Faith In Action Steps

• When my faith begins to feel weak; I will seek advice from the word of God to help me stay strong in my faith
• I will be careful of what I watch and listen to, and be careful to surround myself with faith builders

Prayer of Salvation

The promises of God are yes and amen, but they also belong to the children of God. Therefore, if you are not sure where you stand in your relationship with God and want to be sure you are saved, then recite this prayer of Salvation.

"Dear God, I realize that without Jesus in my life I will not spend eternity with you. I am sorry for the way that I have chosen to live my life. I ask you to forgive me of all my sins. I ask that Jesus would come into my heart and give me the power to live for Him. I ask you to create in me a clean heart and renew my spirit. Lord, I ask you to wash me from all unrighteousness. I freely choose to release my will to you.

You said if I would confess that Jesus is Lord and believe that You raised Him from the dead, I will be saved. Therefore, I declare that I do believe, and I make my confession that You raised Jesus from the dead and I believe Your Word is true.

I thank you for saving me, I thank you for sending Jesus to die on the cross for my sins. Now, in Jesus' name, I renounce the kingdom of darkness where Satan dwells and I ask Your kingdom to come in my life. In Jesus' Name I pray, AMEN."

Now that you have received your free gift of salvation, you need to get into a Bible believing, word teaching church, where you can continue to learn more about Jesus Christ and become more like Him in your everyday life.

Seven things you must do to ensure salvation:

1. Be willing to follow Christ. Luke 9:23; Revelation 22:17; John 7:17
2. Deny self. Luke 9:23; Mark 8:34
3. Take up your cross daily. Luke 9:23, Mark 8:34
4. Follow Christ daily. Luke 9:23, 8:13; Hebrews 3:6-14
5. Lose your life in Christ. Luke 9:24; Mark 8:35
6. Put your relationship with Christ before anything here on earth. Luke 9:25; 1 John 2:15-17; James 4:4; John 15:18-19
7. Don't be ashamed of Christ and His words. Luke 9:26; Mark 8:38

Chapter 1: Increase My Faith

For the sake of understanding, let's define increase. The dictionary defines increase as follows:

- Increase as used with an object is to make greater, as in number, size, strength, or quality; augment; add to.
- To multiply by propagation.

To increase one's faith implies that they have little faith; or not a great belief system in someone or something.

Jesus was teaching His disciples about forgiveness and faith (Luke 17:1-10 NIV), let's look at verses 5-6 below:

In Luke 17:5-6 NIV "The apostles said to the Lord, "Increase our faith!" He replied, "If you have faith as small as a mustard seed, you can say to this mulberry tree, 'Be uprooted and planted in the sea,' and it will obey you.""

Since this set of scripture was teaching on forgiveness, the disciples/apostles, after hearing what Jesus had to say, felt they needed more faith to be able to forgive. Jesus had said to them to forgive their sisters or brother who sin against them each time they repent. Can you imagine how hard it was for the disciples to keep forgiving someone who had wronged them so many times in one day?

Here we are today barely able to forgive one offense in a year! Nevertheless, this command is for us today as well.

So yes, Lord increases our faith to forgive, and to not hold grudges, hatred, or ill-feelings toward the person who wronged us.

We have to remember, the amount of faith is not what is important, it is the genuineness of our faith that matters. The amount of faith is not as important as the right kind of faith. Faith is total dependence on Father God and a willingness to do His will. Faith is powerful! So, you see, we all need to increase our faith to forgive!

Right out the door, James lets us know our faith will be tested. In James 1:2-4 (NIV) he tells us,
"Consider it pure joy, my brothers and sisters, whenever you face trials of many kinds, because you know that the testing of your faith produces perseverance. Let perseverance finish its work so that you may be mature and complete, not lacking anything."

Remember from the last section, we needed to increase our faith to forgive, well, here we see that the pressure will be applied in testing our faith. Using forgiveness as an example of applied pressure, we may feel the pressure to forgive someone and go back to who we were before the incident happened. However, it does not always work that way.

Incidents brings transformation in our lives. God said He will use what was meant to harm us to be for our good (Genesis 50:20 NIV.) In that case, the applied pressure to forgive is null and void if the expectations is to be the way that we were before. The last part of Genesis 50:20 says

"...but God intended it for good to accomplish what is now being done..."

God uses situations to build our character. Without applied pressure we will never truly know what we are able to handle under pressure. We should use those times of pressure as opportunities to grow. So, don't complain about the struggle. Pray through the struggle and ask God to navigate you through it and to increase your faith to believe His Word concerning the situation.

In order for us to use our increased faith we have to walk by faith. James 1:5-8 (NIV) teaches us this. "If any of you lacks wisdom, you should ask God, who gives generously to all without finding fault, and it will be given to you. But when you ask, you must believe and not doubt, because the one who doubts is like a wave of the sea, blown and tossed by the wind. That person should not expect to receive anything from the Lord. Such a person is double-minded and unstable in all they do."

A major increase that is needed for us is wisdom! Wisdom is simply the ability to use practical discernment. This is wisdom to make wise decisions in the face of difficult circumstances. This is the God-given wisdom you can't learn in school. It is given to us in prayer from the almighty God when we ask Him. Lack is the antonym of increase, therefore, when we want our faith increased essentially, we want our wisdom generously increased.

The caveat here is that we must believe and not doubt; completely relying on God. This belief goes beyond just believing in His existence but to the extent that we are believing and expecting that He will hear and answer our prayers when we pray. We cannot have a wavering mindset being moved and tossed by every bad situation. Nor should we ask for unreasonable request, because a heart after God is determined to have the will of God and His desires.

When James speaks of the wavering mind, it refers to a mind that is not completely convinced that God's way is best for them. A wavering mind sees God's word as no more than human advice. Therefore they entertain the option to ignore it and disobey it vacillating with worldly ideologies.

If you are new to the faith walk, weak in your faith or struggling with your faith, one thing for sure is, you can trust God at His word. We have to become loyal to God and confident that God will align us with His perfect will. This is done as we stabilize the wavering mind by committing ourselves wholeheartedly to God.

Faith In Action Steps

Chapter 2: Exercise My Faith

As we consider ways to become committed wholeheartedly to God, we can't help but reflect on what it takes to build muscles in our body. By definition, exercise merely means:

- Something done or performed as a mean of practice or training.
- A putting into action, use, operation or effect.
- A religious observance or service.

With that being said, if we want to increase our faith, then we must exercise our faith. Exercising our faith is inclusive of spiritually eating right and exercising regularly. Eating or feeding our soul with the Word of God and aligning His Word against circumstances is the antidote to exercising our faith. We have to put faith into action!

Hebrews 12:2a (NIV) tells us, "...fixing our eyes on Jesus, the pioneer and perfecter of faith..."

The author, assumed to be Paul, is telling us in this scripture to constantly focus on Jesus, trust in Jesus and not our circumstances. When we put Jesus first and foremost in our lives, then He can perfect, increase and mature our faith.

The world we live in offers many distractions from the faith and could have one believing in a whole lot of stuff that does nothing but diminishes our Christian faith.

When situations happen, they can be used by the Lord to exercise our faith. We get to exercise our belief system in that area of challenge.

This can look differently for everyone as our level of faith varies in the different areas of our life. Examples of exercising our faith:

- Believe and accept the word of God. When we read God's promises and His commands, we believe those words as truth. In doing so, we are exercising our faith.
- Obey the word of God. When we read His commands in the Bible, telling us to do something and we obey it, we are exercising our faith.
- Trust in God's goodness. We have to believe that God is a good God, and everything He gives us is for our good that is when we are exercising our faith.
- Pray God's word back to Him. When we believe God's word, and we pray His word back to Him, He will perform His word on our behalf, that is exercising our faith.
- Meditate on the promises and miracles in God's word. The more we meditate on the word, His promises and the miracles, the more we can believe and trust His word, then we are exercising our faith.
- Defeat doubt with faith. When we speak the word of God over our doubts, then we are exercising our faith.
- Surrender and submit yourself and your mind to God. When we allow the word of God to guide us in our challenges, situations, and circumstances, then we are exercising our faith.

There are many other ways in the word of God to exercise our faith. These are just a few examples to get started.

Knowing that the world offers a lot of distractions as we spoke about earlier, one of the main things we want to do is what it says in Ephesians 6:16 (TPT), "In every battle, take faith as your wrap-around shield, for it is able to extinguish the blazing arrows coming at you from the evil one!"

It is a daily battle to walk in faith, which is why Paul the apostle, encouraged us to TAKE FAITH. He knew that our faith will be a target of the devil and therefore it also became a shield to protect us. Thinking about our physical exercise needs, we had to fight against discouragement, tiredness, time management, etc. So, what more will you have to fight to exercise your faith? In addition to the above list of examples of exercising faith, we can add the following to aide in exercising our faith:

- Consistency in our prayer life. Praying often and as the Lord leads. (1 Thessalonians 5:17)
- Doing devotionals such as Bible reading plans, biblical meditations on the word of God followed by your own essay of what your meditation or devotion spoke to you.
- Encourage others with both words and deeds.

Paul teaches us in 1 Corinthians 2:4-5 (TPT), "The message I preached and how I preached it was not an attempt to sway you with persuasive arguments but to prove to you the almighty power of God's Holy Spirit. For

God intended that your faith not be established on man's wisdom but by trusting in his almighty power."

So, you see, the consistency of prayer, devotions with the Lord and encouraging others with a simple message as Paul teaches will all lend to exercising our faith. The more we do the things required to build our faith the stronger our faith becomes. Then at some point the faith muscle will need to be stretched in order to continue growing.

Faith In Action Steps

Chapter 3: Stretch My Faith

Now that we understand the fundamentals of increasing our faith. Now it's time to figure out and learn how to stretch our faith to believe even more.

Going back to our examples of exercising the muscles in our body, we want to correlate that with exercising our faith to grow beyond what you can see. For example, it is easy to believe God to meet a financial need when we have a good paying job. However, on the other side is learning how to stretch your faith to believe God for your financial needs when you are unemployed or under employed. That is another level of faith.

First, everything we receive from the Lord is by His grace and according to His promises. Therefore, we must know and understand His grace and promises in order for us to believe and trust Him. So, let's go there.

Grace is God's unmerited favor. It is not earned by doing something in particular. It is given to us freely from God. A promise is a covenant or declaration that one would do exactly what they say, or something will happen, just as pledged. The Bible holds many promises for us as believers. So, now that we understand what favor and promise are from a biblical perspective, let's go little deeper into what it means to stretch our faith.

Hebrews 11:1 (TPT) says, "Now faith brings our hopes into reality and becomes the foundation needed to acquire the things we long for. It is all the evidence required to prove what is still unseen."

As we see from this verse, Faith is an action word, it describes what faith does! Faith will *bring* whatever it is that's you are hoping for into reality. So, the question is... What are you hoping for? What are you expecting from God?

Although it is unseen at the moment, does not mean it will remain unseen. The word of God has many promises that we can stand on that will stretch our faith. However, there is something that we must do. We must do Hebrews 11:6 (NIV) that says, "...without faith it is impossible to please God, because anyone who comes to him must believe that he exists and that he rewards those who earnestly seek him."

But how do we do this scripture, you ask? Well, as we earnestly and wholeheartedly seek and come to the Father, trust God and believe in Him and that He exist. He promises and assures us that He will reward us. We should see this as a privilege to come to the Father. But know that faith is a mandatory requirement to properly approach Father God.

Let's take a preview of some Biblical examples of how the power of bold faith worked for some people, keep in mind that "NOW FAITH BRINGS OUR HOPES INTO REALITY:

- Faith moved Abel to choose a more acceptable sacrifice to offer God (Hebrews 11:4).

- Faith translated Enoch from this life, and he was taken up to heaven (Hebrews 11:5).
- Faith opened Noah's heart to receive revelations and warnings from God (Hebrews. 11:7).
- Faith motivated Abraham to obey God's call and leave the familiar to discover territory he was destined to inherit from God (Hebrews 11:8).
- Sarah's faith embraced God's miracle power to conceive even though she was barren and was past the age of childbearing (Hebrews 11:11).
- Faith operated powerfully in Abraham for when he was put to the test he offered up Isaac (Hebrews 11:17).
- The power of faith prompted Isaac to impart a blessing to his sons, Jacob and Esau (Hebrews 11:20).
- Jacob worshiped in faith's reality at the end of his life...imparted a prophetic blessing upon each of Joseph's sons (Hebrews 11:21)
- Faith inspired Joseph and opened his eyes to see into the future (Hebrews 11:22).
- Faith prompted the parents of Moses at his birth to hide him... (Hebrews 11:23).
- Faith enabled Moses to choose God's will... (Hebrews 11:24).
- Holding faith's promise, Moses, abandon Egypt (Hebrews 11:27).
- Faith stirred Moses to perform the right of Passover and sprinkle lamb's blood (Hebrews 11:28).
- Faith opened the way for the Hebrews to cross the Red Sea (Hebrews 11:29).
- Faith pulled down Jericho's wall (Hebrews 11:30).

- Faith provided a way of escape for Rahab the prostitute (Hebrews 11:31).

There is so many others in the Bible that experienced **Active Faith** that would help us to stretch our faith beyond what we can see in front of us. Let us reflect on Hebrews 11:39-40 (TPT) as a means of further stretching our faith. It says, "These were the true heroes, commended for their faith, yet they lived in hope without receiving the fullness of what was promised them. But now God has invited us to live in something better than what they had—faith's fullness! This is so that they could be brought to finished perfection alongside of us."

By now we see that our faith can indeed be stretched beyond what we can see. So, I ask, what will you allow faith to DO in your life?

When we consider stretching our faith, it will be remiss not mention what Jesus has to say.

Mark 11:22-24 (TPT) says this, "Jesus replied, "Let the faith of God be in you! Listen to the truth I speak to you: Whoever says to this mountain with great faith and does not doubt, 'Mountain, be lifted up and thrown into the midst of the sea,' and believes that what he says will happen, it will be done. This is the reason I urge you to boldly believe for whatever you ask for in prayer—be convinced that you have received it and it will be yours."

Jesus did not hold back; He simply tells us to "Let" which means to allow or permit. So here we have to allow or permit faith to work in and through us. Let faith be activated so that it can work in your life. Jesus' instructions to the disciples and to us today is "listen to the truth I speak to you"!

Wow! If He had to tell them to list to the truth that He spoke, then that implies that there were some false words being thrown out there from others. Therefore, in this instance, in order to stretch our faith then we will have to reject false teaching and the world view of situations and receive HIS Truth.

What is the truth Jesus is sharing? He says speak to the mountain with great faith and do not doubt. What is the mountain? It is that thing your fear, the diagnosis you received, the lack of finances, the troubled marriage, the wayward child, the job, career, manager, etc. All of these represent the mountain that must be moved.

When we pray with great faith, powerful things can and will happen for us! All we have to do is believe and receive that what we prayed for will come to pass. The picture that Jesus is painting here of a mountain being tossed into the sea, we know is humanly impossible. The point He is making is, if we have Faith in God, we can accomplish the impossible and the impossible can happen for us.

Let me remind you, Jesus said in Mark 9:23 (NLT), ""What do you mean, 'If I can'?" Jesus asked. "Anything is possible if a person believes."" Do not misunderstand, this is not a genie in the bottle prayer or belief, but quite the contrary it is by FAITH and according to the will of the Father that we can have what we need to serve Him.

Lastly, stretching our faith does not have to be hard or scary, but it does have to be by Faith. This may be a place where you are struggling to believe God for the biggest ask of your life, but I want to encourage you that the word of God is yes and amen. It is truth.

I want to share one of my testimonies. My husband and I went horseback riding a few years ago in Wyoming. Initially, I was eager to jump on the horse but then I changed my mind. He wanted to do it, so I did. Everything was going just fine on the side of the mountain. Then all of a sudden, a hard wind came rushing and spooked my horse, General was his name. He jerked and was about to buck, but I pulled back on the reigns and held him in place. Mind you, he was one of the biggest horses on the trail.

Suddenly, I heard and felt a rip in my right shoulder, I went ouch! The Horse guide asked if I was okay, I said yes. By the time we finished that trip about 40 minutes or so later, I could feel the pain going down my arm. But I have a high tolerance for pain and thought nothing of it. Let me tell you, the next morning I was in tears and literally crying from the excruciating pain. My husband found and took me to an urgent care facility in a nearby town. According to the X-ray, my rotator cup was ripped up in three major places!

Fast forward, we got back home, and I went to see my primary care physician and then a specialist who was bum rushing me to have surgery. He had threats that I would not be able to use my arm without surgery and it will only be usable at a very limited capacity. I replied back to him, I was not comfortable with the surgery and had to pray about it. But he was adamant about the surgery. So, when I finally refused, he seemed to have an attitude. My response was "my God will heal me." He smirked at me and walked out the room.

Well, at this writing it has been over two years, no surgery. I have roughly 95% usage of my shoulder and I can literally do everything that I used to do except maybe throw a softball, which I had no intentions on doing anymore.

How did that happen for me? I trusted God in my healing process. I did a few weeks of physical therapy that was way too expensive. So, the therapist gave me exercises to do at home, which I did. Me and the prayer warriors prayed over my shoulder. I said to the Lord, "You have to heal my shoulder, I have no other alternatives and I trust that You will." I stepped completely out on faith and walked according to the Word of God. I listened to the Lord for any instructions He gave me and did them.

If God did it for me, then He can do it for you! You have a measure of Faith; you just need to stretch it. Faith enabled me to trust the Lord wholeheartedly for the healing of my shoulder. Faith operated powerfully through me to bring healing to my shoulder.

Faith In Action Steps

Chapter 4: Strengthen My Faith

Once our faith is stretched, then it needs to be strengthened. Strengthened means:

- To make or become stronger,
- Give strength to,
- To gain strength,
- To grow stronger.

You may be thinking about all that was said in the last chapter and how you can reach it at this point in your walk with the Lord. You may have been facing a certain challenge for a long time and just learned to live with it or accepted it as your new norm. However, the promises of God can be activated at any point of your life.

Let's review the account of the woman with the issues of blood in Luke 8:43-48 (NLT), "A woman in the crowd had suffered for twelve years with constant bleeding, and she could find no cure. Coming up behind Jesus, she touched the fringe of his robe. Immediately, the bleeding stopped. "Who touched me?" Jesus asked. Everyone denied it, and Peter said, "Master, this whole crowd is pressing up against you." But Jesus said, "Someone deliberately touched me, for I felt healing power go out from me." When the woman realized that she could not stay hidden, she began to tremble and fell to her knees in front of him. The whole crowd heard her explain why she had touched him and that she had been immediately healed. "Daughter," he said to her, "your faith has made you well. Go in peace.""

According to this text we can clearly see that the length of time we deal with an issue does not matter. Whether it has been one year or 12 years, it can be healed, it can be resolved or it can be rectified. What we have to do is be intentional or deliberately touch the hem of Jesus' garment. That is done as we fellowship with the Lord in prayer, fasting, and searching the Bible for His promises and holding fast to them whole-heartily until the manifestation comes. Jesus will feel our heart-felt prayers, worship and seek. Then just as He said to the woman, He can say to us, **YOUR FAITH HAS MADE YOU WELL - YOUR FAITH HAS CHANGED YOUR SITUATION.** Prayer will definitely change a situation and it will change you! This is faith in action!

Building stronger faith takes receiving the truth of God's word. Romans 10:17 (NIV) teaches us, "Consequently, faith comes from hearing the message, and the message is heard through the word about Christ." When the gospel of Jesus is preached, taught, read, listened to, or studied it births righteousness within us that makes us righteous before God. It is not simply because faith is a worthy work and stands alone. It is because faith "receives" the promises declared in the Word of God, that is His atoning work on the cross that is able to save us.

Therefore, the importance of hearing the message of Christ not only saves but it also helps us develop our faith. The more time we spend in the Word of God the stronger our faith becomes. The stronger our faith then the more likely we are to share the Gospel of Christ which in turn strengthens our faith even more.

Why? First, no one shares anything they do not believe in and secondly, what you believe in and trust you will share! So, as Paul writes "consequently" (as a result, effect or outcome), faith comes (progress, arrive in time, be available) from our interacting (to act upon, to participate) with the Word of God.

The enemy do not want you to strengthen your faith. He wants your faith to be weak so that you are unable to lean on, believe or trust the Word of God. That is why it is so hard to pray and read the Bible when you have issues, circumstances, and problems in life.

When we are going through, we have the tendency to push back on prayer and Bible reading. This is the time when we should run to the Bible to strengthen our faith for encouragement and joy. In these times we can lean on James 1:2-4 (TPT) that says, "My fellow believers, when it seems as though you are facing nothing but difficulties, see it as an invaluable opportunity to experience the greatest joy that you can! For you know that when your faith is tested it stirs up in you the power of endurance. And then as your endurance grows even stronger, it will release perfection into every part of your being until there is nothing missing and nothing lacking."

When you are going through difficulties in your life, it is a time when:

- You receive invaluable opportunities to experience great Joy!
- Your faith gets tested!
- That test stirs up your power of endurance!

- Your endurance become even stronger!
- Your strengthen faith releases perfection!
- Faith is released and activated until you have nothing missing or lack for anything!

The Amplified Bible says James 1:4b this way, "...so that you may be perfect and completely developed [in your faith] lacking in nothing." When our faith has been strengthened, we can recall the promises of God readily in situations and defeat the enemy's doubt and unbelief.

Read the following set of scriptures about God's faithfulness out loud so that you may hear the Word of Truth:

- John 14:13-14 And I will do whatever you ask in my name, so that the Father may be glorified in the Son. You may ask me for anything in my name, and I will do it.
- Luke 11:9-13 So I say to you: Ask and it will be given to you; seek and you will find; knock and the door will be opened to you. For everyone who asks receives; the one who seeks finds; and to the one who knocks, the door will be opened. Which of you fathers, if your son asks for a fish, will give him a snake instead? Or if he asks for an egg, will give him a scorpion? If you then, though you are evil, know how to give good gifts to your children, how much more will your Father in heaven give the Holy Spirit to those who ask him!
- Jeremiah 29:12 Then you will call on me and come and pray to me, and I will listen to you.

- Psalm 102:17 He will respond to the prayer of the destitute; he will not despise their plea.
- Psalm 145:18 The Lord is near to all who call on him, to all who call on him in truth.

God is a faithful God, He never changes, He is always true to His word. In fact, Psalm 119:90 (NIV) declares, "Your faithfulness continues through all generations; you established the earth, and it endures."

Be encouraged and know greater is He that is in you than he that is in the world. He promised that He will never leave you or forsake you, but He will be with you until the end of time. He will bring your through every situation and show you how to strengthen your faith so that you will be able to Walk by Faith!

Faith In Action Steps

Chapter 5: Walk By Faith

As our faith is increased, exercised, stretched and strengthened we are enabled to Walk by Faith. While this is a common phrase and people throw it around like candy, we have to learn and understand what it actually means to Walk by Faith.

To Walk by Faith is simply defined as our interaction with God via, prayer, praise, worship, and the study of His word. It is interacting throughout the day with Him, sensing His presence, being empowered by Him and receiving and gaining daily strength and guidance from Him. In order for us to continue to grow in our faith these are the things we should incorporate in our daily lives.

Paul encourages us in 2 Corinthians 5:7 (NIV) "For we live by faith, not by sight." TPT says it this way, "for we live by faith, not by what we see with our eyes." Sight in this text means appearance and Jesus is not in physical form whereas we can "see" Him. Therefore, we have to see Him spiritually, through the eyes of the Word of God.

With that being said, we cannot allow what we see going on in the world to set our standards of living or dictate our spiritual well-being. The building of our faith also builds our confidence in God and His Word. Therefore, we can live out 2 Corinthians 5:8 "...we live in confidence..." knowing at the end of the day, we know where we will spend eternity.

As we learn and continue to Walk by Faith, we must understand that our spiritual growth is directly connected with our walk with God and it is a step-by-step process. This process is governed by the principles of God's word regardless to what the world dictates. The more time spent studying the word of God, the more likely one will be able to follow the Word of God. Remember, faith comes by hearing the word of God.

We cannot afford to attempt to mix the Word with the world. Proverbs 3:5-6 (TPT) teaches us, "Trust in the Lord completely, and do not rely on your own opinions. With all your heart rely on him to guide you, and he will lead you in every decision you make. Become intimate with him in whatever you do, and he will lead you wherever you go."

We see here that we must trust the Lord and essentially trust what the Word has to say and live by it. We also must understand that our own opinions void of God can be dangerous! The Lord wants to guide us but we have to be willing to go in the direction that He prompts us. To be led by the Spirit is a walk of Faith.

Let's see what Apostle Paul teaches us in Galatians 5:16-18 (TPT), "Let me emphasize this: As you yield to the dynamic life and power of the Holy Spirit, you will abandon the cravings of your self-life. When your self-life craves the things that offend the Holy Spirit, you hinder him from living free within you! And the Holy Spirit's intense cravings hinder your self-life from dominating you! So then, the two incompatible and conflicting forces within you are your self-life of the flesh and the new

26

creation life of the Spirit. But when you yield to the life of the Spirit, you will no longer be living under the law, but soaring above it!"

The promise here is that "We will abandon ungodly cravings" because as we walk each moment of each day by faith, then the Spirit of God assures us absolute victory over sinful, worldly desires. To reinforce this, Apostle Paul tells us in 2 Corinthians 1:21 (NIV), "Now it is God who makes both us and you stand firm in Christ. He anointed us," the TPT says it this way "Now, it is God himself who has anointed us. And he is constantly strengthening both you and us in union with Christ." You see, we cannot walk by Faith without the assistance of the Holy Spirit.

Because of the constant strengthening of our faith we can be as Jesus instructed in Matthew 21:21-22 (NIV) that says, "Jesus replied, "Truly I tell you, if you have faith and do not doubt, not only can you do what was done to the fig tree, but also you can say to this mountain, 'Go, throw yourself into the sea,' and it will be done. If you believe, you will receive whatever you ask for in prayer.""

As you recall, the withering of the fig tree in Matthew 21:18-20, represented God's judgement on the unbelieving Israel. Jesus used this illustration to teach the disciples and us, that faith works miracles and is the basis of our answered prayer, without faith it is impossible to please God.

Lastly, Faith is as powerful as we believe in the Lord our God. As I mentioned before, you build your faith by building your relationship with God. This is done by studying/reading the Word of God, trusting God at His word, praying to God and listening for a response, worshipping in song and praises, fellowshipping with other believers and sharing your faith with others. Consistently doing these things, will aide you in increasing your faith, exercising your faith, stretching your faith, strengthening your faith and thereby walking by faith.

Faith In Action Steps

Conclusion

As we come to a close, I want you the reader to be sure you have what you need to increase your faith. Some fundamental aspects of faith are as found in Hebrews 6:1-3 (NKJV), "Therefore, leaving the discussion of the elementary principles of Christ, let us go on to perfection, not laying again the foundation of repentance from dead works and of faith toward God, of the doctrine of baptisms, of laying on of hands, of resurrection of the dead, and of eternal judgment. And this we will do if God permits."

To summarize these scriptures, below are the principles of faith to glean from that will lead you to maturity:

1. Repent from dead works, refers to change a of mind about the demands of the law of Moses. (Hebrews 9:14)
2. Faith directed towards God, referring to leaving dead works that cannot save. (Hebrews 9:14)
3. Baptisms refers to various baptisms, physical and spiritual as found in the new testament scriptures (Acts 19:3-5).
4. Laying on of hands, the impartation of the Holy Spirit and spiritual gifts. (Acts 8:17-19; 19:6)
5. Resurrection of the dead, the resurrection of people during the end times. (Rev 20:11-15; 1 Corinthians 15:12-17)
6. Eternal judgement refers to everyone being judged by the great judge, in which Jesus will determine every believers' reward. (1 Corinthians 3:12-15)

We are tasked with maturity in our understanding, we need to move beyond, but not away from the elementary teaching to a more complete understanding of Faith. Mature Christians should be teaching new Christians the basics, and then acting on what they know. The mature Christians will learn even more from the Word of God by teaching the word of God. There is always a progression in our learning as well as in our faith walk. We measure ourselves with the Word of God not the people around us.

In order to continue to grow in our faith, we also need to live by Ephesians 4:11-16 NIV that says, "So Christ himself gave the apostles, the prophets, the evangelists, the pastors and teachers, to equip his people for works of service, so that the body of Christ may be built up until we all reach unity in the faith and in the knowledge of the Son of God and become mature, attaining to the whole measure of the fullness of Christ. Then we will no longer be infants, tossed back and forth by the waves, and blown here and there by every wind of teaching and by the cunning and craftiness of people in their deceitful scheming. Instead, speaking the truth in love, we will grow to become in every respect the mature body of him who is the head, that is, Christ. From him the whole body, joined and held together by every supporting ligament, grows and builds itself up in love, as each part does its work."

As you are seeking the Lord ask Him to provide you access to the men and women of God who represents the five-fold ministry gifts outlined above. As you see from these verses, it is necessary to obtain teachings from the entire

31

five-fold ministry gifts to reach your fullest potential of **FAITH**.

To this end, I leave you with this prayer from Ephesians 3:14-21 (NKJV):

"For this reason I bow my knees to the Father of our Lord Jesus Christ, from whom the whole family in heaven and earth is named, that He would grant you, according to the riches of His glory, to be strengthened with might through His Spirit in the inner man, that Christ may dwell in your hearts through faith; that you, being rooted and grounded in love, may be able to comprehend with all the saints what is the width and length and depth and height— to know the love of Christ which passes knowledge; that you may be filled with all the fullness of God. Now to Him who is able to do exceedingly abundantly above all that we ask or think, according to the power that works in us, to Him be glory in the church by Christ Jesus to all generations, forever and ever. Amen."

Faith In Action Steps

About the Author

 *Frizella Taylor*

Wife, mother, grandmother, ordained minister, author, conference speaker, writing coach and entrepreneur. Frizella is Pastor and President of Women in Progress Ministries, Inc.

Frizella's writing career began over 20 years ago. She has written and published 13 books to date. She has composed and written various types of books including children's books and devotionals. Her Christian background has provided her with a wealth of leadership experiences (i.e., children's ministry, youth ministry, women's ministry, prayer and intercessory ministry as well as Pastoral) to glean from and share.

Frizella's formal education includes a Master of Science in Information Technology, Bachelor of Science in Management and Business, and an Associate in Computer Programming.

Frizella along with her husband, Steve are owners of TaylorMade Publishing, LLC of Florida (www.taylormadepublishingfl.com) providing services to authors in the areas of coaching, proofreading, editing, formatting, eBook, print book, book promotion videos, and author websites.

Author and Finisher of your Faith

Hebrews 12:2

Book by Frizella

1. Changes, Changes, Changes; GOD Changes You Into the Image of Jesus by HIS Word
2. A Family That Prays - A Book of Prayers
3. Noon Break Into HIS Presence 30-Day Devotional
4. Move From Despondency to Destiny, Your Destiny Awaits
5. Move from Despondency to Destiny Study Guide
6. Mommy Who you Talking to? Teach your Child to Pray (Children's Book)
7. Daddy, What You Reading: Teach Your Child to Study The Bible (Children's Book)
8. Mommy, Daddy What are They Doing: Teach your Child to Worship (Children's Book)
9. Zoo Adventures With Dyamond and Vesta (Children's Book)
10. Write Your Vision Habakkuk 2:2 Note Pad
11. Women Pursuing God With Perseverance Persistence Purpose 31-Day Journey
12. You Are Amazing: The "I AM" Stress Free Coloring Book
13. Jeremiah 29:11 Monthly Motivation & Devotion Journal Calendar

To book Frizella for speaking engagements please email, AuthorFrizellaTaylor@gmail.com